Spawn of the

W. C. Tuttle

Alpha Editions

This edition published in 2024

ISBN : 9789361479427

Design and Setting By
Alpha Editions
www.alphaedis.com
Email - info@alphaedis.com

As per information held with us this book is in Public Domain.
This book is a reproduction of an important historical work. Alpha Editions uses the best technology to reproduce historical work in the same manner it was first published to preserve its original nature. Any marks or number seen are left intentionally to preserve its true form.

I

THE Mohave Indians have a legend of the Calico Mountains and their origin. According to their beliefs, the Great Spirit finished the big task of making the world at this spot.

The desert was the final work of the Great Spirit, and he was much pleased; but in his arms he held a big jumble of rocks, sand and pigments, which were left from the great work. The world was all made and very good to look upon, so he had no place for this extra material.

To get rid of it he simply dropped it at his feet in a mass, and the many-hued pigments spilled over it until the whole was as a bright-hued piece of cloth.

Thus, according to the Indians, was formed these mountains, which are but a jumble of barren rocks, rising sheer from the level desert; scourged through the centuries by the desert sun, wind and sand—an unfading proof that, unlike man, the Great Spirit painted deeper than the surface.

But with all their gaudy colors in the sun, these mountains, at night, are black silhouettes, which appear to be without breadth or thickness; or broken into misty, hazy, unreal piles in the moonlight.

On all sides the desert stretches away to the haze of nothingness—a land of the mirage; scenes which the jealous desert steals from arid lands and holds up to the eyes of desert men to lure them on. Cities, rivers, lakes, with cool, nodding palms, rippling brooks, which seem only a few feet away, then fade out to show a waste of dust-gray mesquite, which rattles in the hot winds, Joshua-trees, with their agonized arms—and sand. Always the sand.

On a rocky plateau of this painted range stood a town—one street of adobe shacks, paved with the solid rock of the mountain. Even the houses were tinted with fantastic colors, where the clay had been mixed with the muck of the silver mines.

At the upper end of the street the cliffs arose sheer for several hundred feet, like gaudy drapes of calico. At the lower end was a succession of broken ledges, which sloped off to the desert, where the winding trails came in from the rest of the world.

To the left of the town was a deep, rocky gorge, so grotesque in formation that it did not appear to be a work of nature. There were natural stone bridges, caves, barriers—unreal in color and design, as though a child-minded giant had modeled them in colored clay and left them to harden in the blistering sun.

This was the residence section of Calico Town, and was known as Sunshine Alley. Just below where the Alley opened onto the desert, on a slight rise of ground, full in the glare of the sun, and with no protection from the ever-sifting sand, was the graveyard, which was known as Hell's Depot. Not a blade of grass, not even a spray of sage grew here. The ground was a mass of small stones, seemingly laid close together like tiles, but showing patterns in colors that would put any man-made mosaic to shame.

One foot deep was the limit of the graves, as the rock below that depth was glass-like flint, but what the graves lacked in depth was made up in height. The mounds of rock were piled until one might believe that the corpse had been of gigantic proportions, or that the sexton wished to preclude any chance of the dead coming back in material form.

Such was Calico in the early 'fifties, when men were gold- and silver-mad. A town of thirty-five hundred population—a population which lived in caves, hollowed places in Sunshine Alley, or picked a corner in the rock and built a rock barrier around them. This gave a roofless dwelling, but rain did not come to Calico, so there was no need for roofs. Water was worth more than whiskey, and morals were as scarce as orchids.

Just now a funeral was in progress, or rather, had been in progress. The corpse was there in the rough casket; the grave was dug and the pall-bearers stood aside, reverently holding their hats in their hands. Clustered around was a cosmopolitan mining-camp audience. Frock-coated, tall-hatted gamblers rubbed elbows with muck-stained miners. Calico-clad wives of miners, children, dogs, and even a group of burros poked onto the flat to add their faces to the mournful proceedings.

Up the desert trail came two men and a lightly-packed burro; all of them gray with the dust and heat. The one who led the caravan was a mighty, weatherbeaten man, with a long, white beard. In appearance he might have been a saint. Surely he could not be a sinner, with the eyes of a dreamer, the nose of a prophet and the beard of a saint; but nature does queer things to disappoint students of physiognomy.

The other man was also tall. His face showed him to be about thirty years of age—a face seemingly hewed from stone, although handsome in its stern mold. His hair was black and he wore it low between his cheek and ear. There was the free, easy swing to his walk, like the half-lope of a desert wolf.

The patriarch halted the caravan on the trail, just short of the street end, and gazed across at the funeral. The younger man glanced over there, with little show of interest.

"Duke," the old man jerked his head toward the graveyard, "I reckon they're plantin' somebody. Let's me and you go over."

They left their burro on the trail and crossed over, attracting little attention. The crowd seemed to be waiting for someone. Two men were standing near the grave, talking earnestly. Suddenly one of them looked up and saw the newcomers. He walked abruptly away from his companion and halted a few feet from the white-bearded man.

"Podner, by yore whiskers yo're a preacher; are yuh?"

The bearded one's right hand came up and slowly stroked the white mass of hair, which hung nearly to his waist-line.

"By my beard," nodded the old man slowly, which neither affirmed nor denied in fact, but seemed to bring joy to the heart of his questioner, who turned on his heel, facing the crowd.

"Folks, we're playin' in luck. The funeral will proceed jist like nothin' happened extraordinary."

"Just a moment, pardner," said the bearded one, "What happens to be the matter?"

"Not a damn thing," laughed the man. "We needed a preacher awful bad—you showed up. There yuh are!"

"Have you no preacher?"

"We did have. Yessir, we shore had a reg'lar one, and he was plumb tidy and slick on funerals—yessir. But he forgot himself complete-like last night when he 'lowed there wasn't no honest rules of averages, which gives him small cards all the time, while 'Ace' Ault get nothin' smaller than kings-up in ten deals."

"Hm-m-m," the white bearded one almost smiled, "Where is this poker-playin' preacher now?"

"Well, hell's delight!" grunted the other. "He's in the casket! We plumb forgot that he couldn't say his own oration. That's where you comes in handy, like a gun in a boot."

The patriarch's head turned slightly and his eyes flashed to the face of his companion, who was regarding him with stony countenance, although the eyes twitched slightly at the outer corners, a sure sign that Duke Steele was greatly amused.

The bearded one crossed to the grave and looked down at the rough coffin, while the audience moved in closer. A burro brayed raucously and two more of the long-eared beasts added their brazen throats to the racket. A miner heaved a rock against the ribs of the nearest beast, and the animal clattered away for a few jumps, looking back solemnly, sadly.

"Friends," the bearded man's voice was deep and musical, as he lifted his bared head and let his eyes travel around the assemblage, "friends, I have been asked to say a few words over the mortal remains of one of God's anointed; a man who has labored in this land of sin and sinners that the Gospel might be brought home to you all. He was fearless in his righteousness; a guide, friend and spiritual counselor.

"He is with you no more, except in spirit, but his many good works will live long after his name has been forgotten. I can see him now—a bulwark of strength to the weak, a solace to the suffering and a friend to all mankind. I can see him——"

"Wait a moment, parson," interrupted the man who had asked the bearded one to deliver the sermon. He stepped forward, hat in hand, clearing his throat apologetically. "I ain't no hand to stop a feller from sayin' what he thinks; but did you know 'Preacher Bill' Bushnell?"

The old man shook his head.

"No, I did not know him, friend."

"I didn't reckon yuh did, parson. We did. I believe in sayin' everythin' good yuh can fer a dead man, but there ain't no use of yuh lyin' to us about Preacher Bill."

The old man glanced down at the coffin, lifted his head slowly and nodded.

"If the Lord is willing, I will take back what I said about him, and start all over again. Wasn't he your minister? Did he not labor among you?"

"He preached," admitted a bearded miner seriously, and added, "when he was sober enough. He owed everybody in Calico, and if he left any good works he sure had 'em cached where nobody'll ever find 'em."

The bearded man nodded slowly and cleared his throat.

"Under those conditions, friends, I suppose I might as well keep away from personalities, and stick to the ordinary burial service. Has anyone a Bible?"

The assemblage looked at each other and back at the bearded one.

"Preacher Bill had one—once," stated a frock-coated gambler. "I dunno what he done with it. If you're a preacher where is your Bible?"

The bearded one glanced quickly at the gambler and held out his hand.

"Let me have a deck of cards, will you?"

"Cards?" queried the gambler, "I have no cards."

"Then you are no better heeled than I am, partner. I have no Bible, you have no cards." He leaned down and placed a hand on the rough casket.

"Preacher Bill, I wish I had known you well enough to have something to say about you. No doubt you were a hard drinker, of very little value to any community, and showed poor judgment in objecting audibly against a run of bad poker luck, but no man can live through childhood and well into life's narrow span without doing some good—leaving somebody better for having known you. Let him who is without sin cast the first stone. Good-by, Preacher Bill."

The bearded man straightened up and looked at the crowd.

"Friends, I ask you to try and remember the good things he has done and forget the bad. We are all children of circumstance. The Bible says, 'The son of man goeth as it is written of him.'

"Whether or not this means that our destiny is all written out in the good book, I do not know. Perhaps poor Preacher Bill merely traveled according to what had been written of him—powerless to do otherwise. Shall we say that he was unfit? I think that is all I can say."

"Parson," one of the miners stepped out of the crowd and held out his hand to the old man, "if you start a church here, I'll sure as hell go to hear yuh preach."

The old man smiled sadly, shook hands with several of the miners and turned back to where Duke Steele stood. They looked closely at each other, turned and went back to their burro, without a word; while the mortal remains of Preacher Bill Bushnell were lowered one foot deep into Hell's Depot and piled high with heavy stones.

"Le Saint," said Duke Steele, as they plodded toward the street, "I wonder what will be said over your remains?"

The old man turned his head and glanced back toward the group at the cemetery.

"I wonder, Duke. Perhaps I shall be lucky enough to have my funeral oration spoken by a man who did not know me any better than I knew Preacher Bill. Will he say, 'This is Paget Le Saint,' or will he say 'The Saint?' I wonder. Still, what should I care, Duke?"

"Damn little difference it makes, after a man's dead," nodded Duke Steele.

"True as Gospel, Duke. Life is the only thing that interests me; death I know nothing about—nor care."

And the Saint spoke truly, when he said he did not care; for the Saint was a fatalist, a gambler, who staked his life against other men's gold. Just as surely as Kidd and Morgan were pirates of the seas, the Saint was a pirate of the Desert, whose appearance belied his calling. Men seemed to speak softly in his presence, as though awed by the majesty of his face and great white beard. Oaths never passed his lips and no man had ever seen him take a drink of liquor. He censured no man for doing evil, and his open philosophy of life fitted in well with the rough lands of the West.

No man, except Duke Steele, knew the real business of the Saint, and he knew only because they were of a kind. Duke Steele was a gunman, a killer, a gambler, and he, alone, knew that the Saint was all of these. An old wolf in the raiment of a sheep; as resourceful and dangerous as an old wolf, and with the brain of a Solomon.

But no man, not excepting Duke Steele, knew anything more about the Saint than they had observed from contact with him, for he confided in no man. He had wandered much, and at times would mention distant parts of the country.

Names seemed to interest him greatly—names of men. It was as though he was always searching for a certain name, which he could only remember by hearing it spoken. Duke Steele wondered at times if the Saint was not just a trifle insane.

For he was a strange personality at times; given to brooding, violence, turning in a flash to extreme kindness and good humor. He often spoke his own name, as though mocking himself. But of his ancestry, his early life, he made no mention.

Duke Steele had been one of his gang in a raid on the Cohise mines, which had been skilfully planned and executed, and without the loss of a man.

Three weeks before the Saint's outfit had boasted of twelve men. Where the other ten were now could only be told by a bunch of Apaches, who ambushed them beyond the Colorado. The Saint and Duke Steele were the only ones to escape.

The plunder of the Cohise mining camp had been taken by the Indians, and the Saint and Steele were forced to be content with saving their lives and one burro. But Steele was an optimist and the Saint did not care for money. It meant nothing to him.

Men believed him insane, at times, because of his total disregard for wealth. He would nurse a sick man with all the tenderness of a woman, or kill a malcontent with the cold-bloodedness of a tiger. But travel, he must. His eyes ever turned toward the hills, as though he was wondering what was on the other side. A prospector had told them of Calico, and to Calico they had come, with not a drop of water nor a crumb of food left.

"The Lord must be looking out for us," observed Duke Steele, as they herded their burro up the main street.

"Fate," corrected the Saint. "The Lord has nothing to do with this place, Duke. It looks like the devil might have located it, did one or two assessments, and relinquished it on account of the heat."

A man crossed the street ahead of them and the Saint stopped him with the question, "Friend, can you tell us where we may find lodging?"

"Lodging?" The man parroted the word. "There ain't a hotel in Calico. Better see Sleed, I reckon. Since Preacher Bill got killed there's a vacant hole in Sunshine Alley, and maybe yuh can rent it from Sleed."

"And who is Sleed?" asked the Saint.

"Who?" The man looked curiously at them. "Yuh must be strangers in this part of the country if yuh don't know who Sleed is. He's the big man around here.

"Owns the Silver Bar saloon over there, and owns the California at Cactus City. Owns the Lady Slipper and the Nola mines, which are the biggest producers here. Sleed was one of the original locators, and he sure does own this town, y'betcha."

"He owns the hole yuh spoke about?" queried Steele.

"Yep—owns most all of the Alley. You just ask for Silver Sleed over at the Silver Bar saloon. 'S funny yuh never heard of Silver Sleed."

"No doubt," nodded the Saint. "Our sources of information appear very lax in not apprising us of this great personage. Still, it is never too late to meet the great. We both thank you, friend."

The Saint turned the burro toward the front of the Silver Bar saloon, while their informant shuffled his feet in the gravel street and wondered whether or not the old patriarch was making fun of him. The Saint was not over fifty years of age, but looked seventy.

Silver Sleed was a giant of a man, with a great black beard, which grew almost to his eyes; eyes that reflected a greenish light, like the sheen of jade. He wore his hair long, after the fashion of the time, and his clothes were a trifle extreme, but befitted his occupation and position as the richest and most powerful man in the country. The law had never penetrated the

Calico hills, so Silver Sleed set himself up as judge and arbiter, from which there was no appeal. In all cases which did not directly or indirectly affect himself or his interests, he was fair in his decisions.

The Silver Bar saloon was not a pretentious place, being one story high, built of adobe, but it was the largest building in Calico. The floor space was about forty feet wide by sixty feet deep, which was taken up by a long bar, gambling layouts and a dance floor. It was the only saloon in Calico, which was conclusive evidence that Sleed owned the town.

Calico spoke many languages, but among this polyglot of tongues, only one, Louie Yen, spoke Chinese. Sleed did not like Chinese, so he limited the camp to Louie Yen, who was a "velly good laundly—yessum." Louie was so old that he claimed to remember the time when Ruby Hill was nothing but a hole in the ground; old and very wise, after his own fashion.

But no man may rule a community without assistance. Sleed surrounded himself with a few trusted men, who were paid for doing certain things without asking the why and wherefore; men who might be undesirable to a village of God-fearing folk, but passing unnoticed in Calico, where, according to the parlance of Sunshine Alley, everything went, except the cook-stove and one joint of pipe.

Just now Sleed was standing with his back to the bar, in the saloon, his eyes squinted, as though in deep thought. Beside him stood a slender, dark-featured man, dressed in the habiliments of the professional gambler. His black eyes were sullen and shifty, and his long fingers moved nervously at his sides, as he flashed a sidewise glance at Sleed.

"That's your idea of a square deal, is it, Sleed?"

Sleed turned his head and looked coldly at the gambler.

"Ace Ault, this ain't no deal. You killed Preacher Bill because—well, not because he said yuh dealt a crooked game, but because yuh was jealous."

"Jealous, hell!" snapped Ault. "He said——"

"I know what he said," interrupted Sleed coldly. "It gave yuh the chance yuh wanted, Ault. Preacher Bill was a dirty old bum and his tongue was against him, but he was educatin' Luck. He was smart, and he was learnin' her a lot of things. She liked him."

"And because I protected my honor against his lying tongue I've got to leave the camp, eh?" queried Ault sarcastically.

"Honor?" Sleed laughed into his beard. "Honor? Good God, when did a tinhorn like you get any honor?"

Ault's face went a trifle darker, and he lifted his hands to a level with his waist.

"You travel *muy pronto*," snapped Sleed. "Better go north, Ault, so yuh won't have any reason even to pass Calico town again."

"Think so?" snapped Ault. His right hand flashed up from under his coat. From across the room came the jarring thud of a pistol shot, and Ault jerked back, firing his pistol a foot over Sleed's head. For a moment Ault's eyes shifted around the room, as he grasped at the bar for support, half-turned toward the door and fell sprawling.

One of Sleed's men came slowly across the room, pistol in hand, watching Ault closely. Sleed's expression had not changed.

"Quick work, Loper," he said softly. Loper nodded and shoved his gun back into its holster.

Just then the Saint and Duke Steele came into the door. Sleed looked at them indifferently, and motioned for some more men to assist in carrying Ault's body out of the place. The Saint and Steele stood aside and watched the men file out.

"Silver Sleed?" asked Steele.

Sleed looked at him for a moment; glanced toward the door as he nodded. Some of the men who had been at the graveyard were coming in, looking curiously back at the men carrying Ace Ault.

"We're lookin' for a place to live in," said Steele. "A man told us to see Silver Sleed."

"Yeah?" Sleed squinted at the Saint and back to Steele.

"Whatcha goin' to do in Calico?"

"You didn't expect an answer to that, did yuh?" asked Steele, with a smile.

Sleed grunted softly. One of the men from the graveyard stepped in and spoke to Sleed.

"The graybeard's a preacher, Sleed. He said a few things for Preacher Bill, and they was damn well said, after he got put right."

Sleed looked at the Saint curiously, and found the Saint looking straight at him. Something in that glance seemed to bother Sleed. It was as though this tall, white-bearded, hawk-eyed man was peering into things that Sleed did not want anyone to see. Sleed glanced down at the floor for a moment and nodded.

"I reckon there's places to live in. Yuh can have Preacher Bill's place or yuh can have—" Sleed looked up and glanced toward the door—"I think yuh can have the place where Ace Ault lived."

"We both thank you, sir." The Saint's voice boomed like the deep notes of a pipe-organ.

Sleed glanced quickly at him and saw that the Saint's eyes were closed, as though he had shut out material things while he thought deeply.

"I'll show 'em the places, Sleed."

It was the miner who had offered to come to church in case the Saint would do the preaching. Sleed nodded and turned back to the bar, but he watched the three men go out of the door.

"Loper, who are them two men?" he asked.

"I dunno." Loper shook his head.

"Find out."

Sleed turned back to the bar and called for whiskey. For some unknown reason he was worried. The killing of Ault amounted to nothing. He discarded that as a possible reason for his unrest. Was it the white-bearded man? Sleed scowled at his glass of liquor for a moment and placed it back on the bar untasted.

II

THE Saint and Steele found that there was little choice between the two dwellings, but they selected the one made vacant by the death of Preacher Bill. It was a roofless, windowless, rock hut about ten feet square, built in an angle of the canyon which supplied two of the walls. An open fireplace was used for cooking, and the utensils were either placed on rock shelves or on the ground.

Preacher Bill's blankets were still spread from his last night's sleep, but the larder was empty.

"I reckon yuh can get along," said their guide. "I'm Jim Cates, but most everybody calls me 'Mica.' 'S I said before, if yuh start preachin', I'm goin' t' have a front seat."

He started away, but turned back.

"Say, if yuh get a call to speak over the remains of Ace Ault, I can tell yuh a few things to make yore oration easier. Ault was crooked as a snake in a cactus patch. He never———"

Mica Cates stopped talking and cleared his throat. A girl had come up near the doorway and was looking at them. She was about twenty years of age, fairly well dressed. A pair of big, brown eyes, misty with tears, looked at them from a cameo-like face, which was framed in a mass of brown hair. Her cheeks were streaked with tear-marks and her lips quivered as she looked around. Then she turned, without a word, and disappeared around the canyon wall.

"Sleed's daughter," said Cates softly. "Her name is Nola, but Sleed said she was his luck so many times that everybody calls her Luck."

"Been cryin'," said Steele wonderingly.

"Uh-huh. Mebbe yuh didn't see her down to Hell's Depot. She was there. I reckon she was the only one to care about Preacher Bill. Yuh see, she ain't had no chance to learn book teachin's, until Preacher Bill took to learnin' her. He was eddicated a lot, and she sure wanted to learn."

Steele nodded. "She's a mighty pretty girl, Cates."

"And 'nother thing," said Cates softly, "yuh don't want to have nothin' t' do with her. Sleed's a killer, where Luck's concerned. Mebbe that's one reason why Ault got a ticket for the Depot. Jist let her alone and don't cross Silver Sleed, and you'll git along here. What did yuh say yore names was?"

The Saint held out his hand and Cates shook hands with him, flinching from the crushing grip of the Saint's hand.

"We both thank you, Mica Cates," boomed the Saint. "If I preach in Calico town I shall deem it a pleasure to see you in the front row."

Mica Cates bobbed his head and hurried away. He flexed his right hand and shook his head.

"My Gawd, I never knowed a preacher with a grip like that—nossir! I didn't find out their names and I'm danged if I'd ever ask any man twice."

Cates climbed back up the rocky trail to the street, where he met Loper.

"Where did they hole up?" asked Loper.

"Preacher Bill's place."

"Ask 'em their names, Mica?"

"Y'betcha, I did."

"What names did they give yuh?"

Mica Cates glanced back down the trail, wiped the perspiration off his brow with the back of his hand.

"They ain't givin' away names, I reckon."

"Yuh asked 'em, didn't yuh?" snapped Loper angrily.

"Y'betcha, I did. Mebbe they didn't hear me—I dunno."

Loper hitched up his belt and strode back to the street. It was very hot and he had no desire to climb down into Sunshine Alley and argue about names.

III

"WE'VE got a home," said Duke Steele dubiously, as he leaned against the rough stone doorway, squinting in the reflected light from the desert sun; "but when we got there the cupboard was bare."

"Yes," nodded the Saint, "but how long have we fasted, Duke? Since breakfast." He pointed at the hills above them, dotted with tunnels, where a host of men drove into the bowels of the earth. Came the dull jar of blasting, the rattle of falling rock from the ever-growing dumps.

"Men are toiling up there, Duke; while down on the street another group of non-toilers are planning to get the fruits of that labor, without toil. You and I do not toil; therefore we must use our brains to devise ways and means to get the necessary provender."

"Just about how?" queried Duke.

The Saint unrolled some of his meager belongings on the stone floor, and in the center of it all was a small package. The Saint picked this up and got to his feet.

"Duke, it has been seldom that I have had to stoop to their use, but when I am forced to such an extremity they never fail."

"Meaning what?" smiled Duke.

The Saint unrolled the small package and held in his hand two halves of a walnut; empty of all meat, and polished to a mahogany finish. In one of the halves was a polished black object, about the size of a garden pea.

"The tools of a cheap gambler," said the Saint, studying Duke's dubious expression. "Yet one must be dexterous and have the courage of his calling."

"Where does the game come in?" asked Duke.

The Saint knelt down on a blanket, smoothed it out and placed the two shells open side down. He slipped the black pea under one of the shells, and with a rapid twist of his hand and fingers, shuffled the shells for a moment.

"Which one is it under, Duke?" he asked.

Duke indicated the one and the Saint lifted the shell. There was no pea under it. The Saint repeated the process slower this time, and Duke Steele was willing to bet his neck on picking the right shell, but he was mistaken.

"Is it under the other shell, Saint?" he asked.

"That is hardly a fair question, Duke. Just supposing I had opened my game, and a bettor had picked the other shell. Would it be good policy to have the pea under that shell? In our financial condition we cannot afford to take any great chances, and I know of no smaller chances of losing than by operating the two little walnut shells."

Duke nodded shortly. "I reckon that's right, Saint. Looks to me like Sleed has this place under his thumb. I suppose he's got every gunman working for him, which makes it a poor place for us."

The Saint placed the two shells in his pocket and came to the doorway. The setting sun slanted against the expanse of Ruby Hill, bringing out a myriad of colors, until the whole land seemed to be a vast drop-curtain of fantastic shades. The voices of men drifted down to them as clear cut as the tinkling of bells. The rasp of a pick, the clank of hammer on steel seemed to come from the air above them and at no great distance.

And like the dimming of a great light the sun moved its rays swiftly up the side of the mountain, leaving in its track a misty softness, almost as blue as moonlight. Blast after blast seemed to jar the world, as the last shots of the afternoon were fired. A few moments later, like ants coming from their burrows, the men came from their tunnels and down the steep hillside, while from Sunshine Alley the supper fires sent up long, straight streamers of smoke to signal them home.

"Men will always toil," said the Saint, as though talking to himself. "Toil day after day until their span of life is done, and after them their sons will take up the toil and carry it on. And what does it all mean? Will the work that these men are doing amount to anything in the final scheme of things? Will the sweat of their brows and the callouses on their hands mean anything?"

"Is there a reason for things, I wonder, Duke?" He turned and put his hand on Steele's shoulder. "I have no conscience, no morals. I have killed, like the wolf kills, and yet I have no fear of death—only wonder.

"I have studied men from the frozen North to the tropics. I know their different breeds, languages, customs. I have seen a Cree chief die, and I have seen the passing of a Yaqui brave. I have seen the mystery of the unknown come into the eyes of a learned man, and I have held the wrist of a dying degenerate. They all die alike, Duke. Never have I seen a man who did not fight against the death, and I have never seen one pass into the borderland with a smile of welcome. Always that mystery.

"Sometimes I wonder if death is a punishment. The fear of death is punishment to most men, no matter who they are. A minister of the Gospel fights against the hand of death as strongly as the worst sinner ever bred, and why? The hereafter is a mystery—life is just as great a mystery."

Duke nodded, solemnly. "I reckon you're right, Saint. I kinda feel sorry for Sleed's girl."

The Saint looked down at the rocky floor and smiled in his great beard.

"Life is no mystery to youth, and you are only thirty years of age, Duke. But don't feel sorry for Sleed's girl. In the first place, she is Sleed's girl; in the second place, you are Duke Steele."

Duke swung away from the doorway and looked up the hill toward the town. He turned and looked at the Saint.

"I—I reckon you're right, Saint. I kinda forgot."

IV

"IT CAN'T be beat, friends. The more you put down, the less you take up. Never buck another man's game, because it was not invented to lose money for its owner. The gent bets five that he can pick the right shell.

"One at a time, gents. This is a one man game, unless you both want to bet on the same shell. Empty again, gents. Where's the next man who is foolish enough to think he can beat a sure-thing game?"

The Saint's voice boomed softly as he pocketed the bet and slowly moved the two walnut shells. The yellow light from the Silver Bar windows lit up his white hair and white beard, as he lifted himself to his full height and studied the crowd in the street.

The Saint had secured a small, rough table, which he had placed in the street, using the lights from the saloon to illuminate his game. A big moon, peeping over Ruby Hill, lit up the street in a soft blue haze, broken by the blocky shadows of the rough buildings, and shot here and there by the yellow lights from oil lamp or candle.

The narrow street was thronged with people, for Sunshine Alley moved to the main street at night. Money was plentiful, and the toilers threw it away, living only in the present.

The shell game was new to Calico, and Calico was anxious to welcome something new. Men jostled each other for a chance to place a bet; while the Saint's voice boomed a warning to each and all.

"It can't be beat, brother. The hand is quicker than the eye. Another empty shell."

"Don't nobody ever win?" asked a miner.

"Nobody, brother. Again I say to you all, it can't be beaten."

The crowd laughed. It was unusual for a game-keeper to declare that no one can beat his game. The Saint was deadly serious, and this amused the crowd. Another man, who had watched several bets swept from the table, moved in and tossed several gold pieces beside the shells.

"Pick up your money, friend," urged the Saint. "You can't win. Might as well toss your money into the dust and walk away from it. All right, if you insist. Thank you for the present."

The man turned away and went toward the saloon door. Duke Steele had been watching the game and now he moved in closer to the Saint, who dug into his pocket and handed Duke a fistful of money.

"Take a spin at the wheel, son. I don't want to take all of Silver Sleed's business away from him."

"I reckon Sleed can stand it better than we can," laughed a miner, who had donated liberally to the elusive black pea.

Duke moved out of the crowd and started for the saloon door, when he came face to face with Sleed's Luck. The girl was standing on the raised step of the saloon watching the crowd around the Saint, but now she looked straight at Duke, who removed his sombrero slowly. He wanted to speak to her, but turned and started on into the Silver Bar, realizing that he had never met her.

"Wait," she said softly, and he stopped. Loper came out of the door and walked to the edge of the steps, looking toward the crowd in the street.

"You wanted to speak to me?" asked Duke.

"Yes, I want to speak to you—about—him." She motioned toward the Saint as she spoke.

"My pardner?" queried Duke.

"Yes. I—I heard him at the graveyard today. Is he a preacher?"

"He can preach," said Duke slowly.

"He has been educated," said the girl, as though talking to herself. "He must know a lot of things."

"Yes'm, he sure does," nodded Duke, and might have added that the Saint would have been hanged many times for divulging even a part of what he knew.

"I wonder if I could talk to him," she said quickly. "Not tonight—tomorrow—maybe."

"Yes'm, I reckon yuh could. We're livin' where Preacher Bill used to live."

Luck nodded. "I saw you there. Preacher Bill was my friend. What is his name?" She motioned toward the Saint.

"Le Saint."

"Le Saint," she said softly. "I thought of him that way when I saw him at the graveyard. My father let Preacher Bill teach me things, and I wonder—my father is down at Cactus City tonight."

"You've lived here a long time?" asked Duke.

"Two years."

"Mighty long time to live here," observed Duke.

Luck nodded slowly. "A long time—yes. Nothing but heat in the day and this—" She gave a weary gesture toward the street—"at night. I have lived in the North, where the mountains are big and cool; where there are big trees and rivers. It is never cool here. At times it is a dreary cold—then the heat."

Duke nodded and looked up at the moon, hanging like a great ball only a short distance above the hill. Suddenly an altercation started across the street beyond the crowd around the Saint. A babble of voices, a curse, shrilled in a woman's voice—a shot.

Duke turned quickly to Luck, but she had disappeared in the crowd. A man elbowed his way across the street, laughing as he reached the door, and spoke to Loper.

"Woman fer a change, Loper. 'Tejon Mary' tried to knife a feller, but he was lookin' fer it and shot her."

"'S time somebody stopped her," grunted Loper. "She was loco. Sleed was goin' t' ship her out, anyway."

The crowd around the shell game began to scatter and look for another diversion. Duke went out to the Saint, whose pockets were bulging with money.

"Game is closed," said the Saint, putting the shells in his pocket and picking up the table, "and again we have a stake."

He placed the table in the alleyway between the Silver Bar and the adjoining building.

"I was surprised not to have Silver Sleed try to stop my game," said the Saint, as he joined Duke.

"He's in Cactus City tonight, Saint. I had a talk with his daughter."

"Sleed's Luck?"

"Yeah."

"Son, it is none of my business—" began the Saint, but Duke stopped him, and the Saint listened closely while Duke told him what the girl had said.

He shook his white beard slowly when Duke finished.

"I reckon," said Duke slowly, "I reckon you've just about got to start in where Preacher Bill left off."

"Tomorrow," mused the Saint. "Tonight I would refuse to consider it; tomorrow is another day. A man is a fool to declare his intentions more than one minute into the future. Let us procure food, Duke Steele, after that we will sleep. It has been a long day."

From within the saloon came the squeak of a fiddle, the tinpanny rattle of a piano, the scrape of boots. The dance had begun. Several men were going down the street, carrying a blanketed figure which had been Tejon Mary—who was loco. From far out in the barren hills a coyote yapped dismally.

Sleed came back from Cactus City the next day; came back like a sore-headed grizzly looking for trouble. He had drunk heavily, played poker all night, and the heat of the day had ground his temper to a razor edge.

Men kept away from Silver Sleed when he was in this humor, but he soon heard of the shell game, which had held the attention of the crowd the night before, and his face purpled with rage. He cursed everyone in sight and sent for Loper, who was almost as sore-headed as his master.

Sleed took him to the rear of the room, sat him down at a table and demanded an explanation.

"How could I stop him?" demanded Loper. "I ain't Sleed. The crowd liked his game, 'cause he told 'em all that it can't be beat."

"How much did he win?" growled Sleed.

"I dunno. Prob'ly about two hundred dollars. Tejon Mary got shot, and that kinda busted up the crowd."

Sleed leaned back and licked the edge of a frayed cigar, while he waited for Loper to explain more.

"I seen Luck talkin' to the other fellow."

Sleed snapped the cigar aside and leaned across the table.

"Luck was talkin' to this old man's pardner?"

"Yeah."

"What about?"

"I dunno all they talked about, Sleed. I didn't want to move in too close, but I know she was askin' him about the old man."

"About the old man," parroted Sleed. "What did she want to know about him?"

"I dunno."

"You dunno," mimicked Sleed. "Is there anythin' you do know? Wasn't your ears workin'?"

"I told yuh I didn't want to move in close, Sleed. I heard some of it and——"

"Oh, you heard some of it, did yuh?" Sleed got ponderously to his feet and leaned both hands on the table, as he snarled down at Loper. "You heard some of it, but you don't know what they talked about."

Loper licked his lips and wished that the interview was over.

"Luck asked him what the old man's name was and——"

"What was it?" snapped Sleed.

"Le Saint."

Silver Sleed stared down at Loper; stared curiously, vacantly. He lifted one hand and brushed it across his lips, while his fixed gaze seemed to look through Loper and beyond. Loper shifted nervously, but Sleed continued to stare.

Suddenly he jerked, like a man awaking from sleep, and sat down slowly in a chair.

"Le Saint," he muttered softly.

"Funny first name," said Loper slowly. "Paget, I think he called it. Must be a furriner."

Silver Sleed did not seem to hear him.

"I dunno what the other feller's name is, but he sure looks like he could take care of himself. Packs a gun that looks like it had been used a-plenty; and he's got the walk of a cat. The old man's gun ain't no ornyment either. Mebbe he's a preacher—I dunno."

Sleed continued to stare at the table-top.

"Want me to pack a talk to him?" asked Loper. "I can tell him to put out of here, or that he can't run no game in Calico."

"No." Sleed shook his head slowly and leaned closer to Loper. "Do yuh know anythin' about that shell game?"

"Only that it can't be beat."

"Of course it can't," admitted Sleed hoarsely. "That pea ain't under either shell. Suppose that you bet a lot of money on the pea bein' under one of them shells, and it wasn't there, and yuh grabbed the other one and found it empty?" Sleed grinned wolfishly. "What would yuh do, Loper?"

"That's it, eh?" grunted Loper. "I reckon I'd take my money back."

"Which might start trouble."

"Thasall right," grunted Loper. "I'd be lookin' for trouble."

Sleed got to his feet and jerked his head toward the bar, as an invitation to have a drink.

"Let this man set up his game tonight, if he wants to. I reckon you know what to do, Loper."

Loper nodded. "Uh-huh. But have somebody watchin' this other feller, Sleed; he's dangerous, y'betcha."

"Some of the boys will take care of him. Maybe I'll watch him myself."

Sleed spilled his liquor in the pouring, but filled his glass to the brim, while Loper wondered what had happened to Steed's iron nerve. He wondered if his boss were losing his nerve, or if it were only the effects of too much liquor and loss of sleep.

"Got any more orders for today?" asked Loper.

Sleed shook his head, splashing the liquor from his glass into his beard. Then he tossed the half-empty glass over the bar and walked out of the door.

"Guess that whisky don't set well on his stummick today," observed the bartender, kicking the broken glass aside.

"Somethin' don't," admitted Loper seriously.

"He's drinkin' too much, I reckon."

"You better mention it to him," grinned Loper. "He's in good shape for a temp'rance lecture right now."

"'F he ever gets snakes——"

"It'll be hell on the snakes," finished Loper.

V

LONG strings of mules, driven with a jerk-line, and hauling heavy, clumsy ore wagons, drifted out of Sunshine Alley, hauling great loads of silver ore to the mills at Cactus City, fifteen miles away. It was a hard journey across the desert to Cactus City, but water was necessary for the handling of the ore—and Calico had none. Many of the wagons brought back great casks of water to supply Calico. There was no ice. The cool of the evening lowered the temperature of the water a trifle, but a cold drink was unknown in Calico town in summer.

Duke Steele and the Saint had stocked their larder from one of the stores and had secured several badly-needed blankets. A passing wagon had sold them a small cask of water at a large price, but they were willing to pay. The burro had joined forces with several more of its kind, which were trying to eke out a living in the Alley by devouring anything and everything from an old newspaper to a much-boiled bone. At times, as though by signal, they would all bray together, their raucous voices echoing brazenly from the cliffs.

Mica Cates came down the road and stopped at sight of Duke and the Saint.

"They took Ault and Tejon Mary to Cactus City," he announced. "Ault had some friends in Cactus, and Sleed didn't want Mary buried here." Cates laughed and added, "Mebbe Sleed was afraid Mary's ghost might not be welcome among so many good ones."

"Is Cactus City any better than Calico?" asked Duke.

"Better morals," nodded Mica. "They don't have a killin' down there more'n once a week. You stay here and you'll find a-plenty of funerals to work on. Ain't no money in it as far as I can see, but Preacher Bill had a system. He orated at funerals fer nothin' quite a while, and one day he whittled out a cross and fastened it to a headstone. She looked kinda pious. A gambler, who was religious as hell, saw him put up this here cross, so the gambler takes up a collection fer old Bill. I reckon he got a hundred dollars fer him, and after that old Bill packs a cross with him all the time and hopes for a killin'."

Cates grinned and went on up the road. He was like a daily paper to Calico, and spent most of his time retailing news, picking up new items at each stop and telling hearsay as personal experience.

Duke Steele turned from watching Cates and saw Luck coming slowly down the trail toward their adobe. The Saint glanced up at the girl and back at Duke, who was smiling at her. She came shyly up to them and Duke introduced her to the Saint. She was even prettier in the harsh light of day than in the dim lights of the night before.

"I—I wanted to talk to you," she faltered, looking at the Saint. She traced a pattern with her toe in the sand and seemed undecided just what else to say.

"I think I understand," nodded the Saint. "You want to learn and you think I am capable of teaching you. Is that it?"

"Yes," eagerly. "Preacher Bill taught me—some. But he's gone now—and I—I wondered. He wasn't a good man like you, but he wanted to help me. You see, I have never been to a regular school."

The Saint turned his head slowly and looked at Duke Steele. Somehow it did not seem funny to them. The Saint turned back to her and said, "And why do you think I am better than Preacher Bill?"

"I don't know," she admitted softly, "I don't know how I know you are—but I do. Preacher Bill had a Bible, with pictures in it, and you look like one of them. Preacher Bill said it was the picture of a saint."

The Saint lifted his head and stared up the Alley, shutting his eyes against the glare of the reflected light, while the girl watched him eagerly. He turned and looked at her.

"Why don't your father send you where there are schools? He can afford it."

Luck shook her head.

"Preacher Bill wanted him to send me away, but he only laughs and says he can't afford to lose his luck. He says I bring him luck. I guess he believes this. He talks about it so much that nobody ever calls me Nola any more."

"Where is your mother, child?" asked the Saint.

Luck shook her head.

"I don't know. Dad never talks about her, and when I ask him he gets angry. I don't remember her. I remember that we lived in the North, where it gets cold, and where there are big mountains. Since then we have traveled all over the country—Dad and I."

"You ain't had much of life, that's a cinch," muttered Duke. "Feller hadn't ought to drag a girl over the country like that. Bad enough for a boy."

Luck shut her lips tightly for a moment, and then, "I guess I can stand it. Dad says he is going to get me some books. Ace Ault wanted to get me some, but Dad put a damper on that idea. Dad didn't like Ace."

"Perhaps your dad won't like me," suggested the Saint.

"Well—" Luck hesitated a moment, "I'll tell him about you, and—will you teach me, if he don't mind?"

The Saint looked quizzically at her, and his eyes shifted to a far-away look, as though he were undecided. Then he nodded.

"Yes, child—if he don't mind."

Luck turned quickly and ran up the trail, as though she was going to lose no time in finding out. Duke smiled after her and looked at the Saint, who was staring down at the ground, his hands clenched at his sides. The face of a saint was gone now, and in its stead was the grinning snarl of an old wolf. He lifted his face and looked at Duke Steele, who was staring at the change in the old man's face and manner.

"Duke Steele—" the Saint's voice was thin, almost a whine—"I've lived to kill—kill, do you hear me? Now, I've promised—God, why did I——?"

He swung his head as though in pain, and walked away. Duke watched him going slowly down the road, his shoulders hunched, as though the weight of the world rested on his back.

Whom did he live to kill? Why did his promise to Luck change his whole being? Duke frowned and tried to gather some reason for the old man's feelings, but in vain. The Saint left the road and climbed the hill to a pinnacle of rock, where he sat and stared down the canyon, chin in hands, like a great, white-headed eagle watching for its prey.

It was an hour later that the Saint came back. He seemed older, whiter and very tired. Duke made no mention of what had passed between them, and the Saint did not open the subject. He sat down in the doorway and examined his revolver—an old single-action Colt .45, scarred and polished from much usage. His long, lean fingers seemed to caress the old gun lovingly. There were no notches on the butt of this old gun, but Duke Steele knew that its muzzle had spouted death many times.

Suddenly Duke spoke.

"Saint, what made you old before your time?"

"Old? Before—my—time?" The Saint turned his head and looked at Duke.

"Uh-huh. You ain't over fifty, are yuh? You ain't got no right to wear long white hair and whiskers and make folks think you're as old as the hills."

The Saint ran his hand under his beard and lifted it in range of his eyes. For several moments he peered at it, as though he had never seen it before.

"Duke, what would I look like without this beard?"

"I ain't got the slightest idea, Saint. It sure does cover your face and head."

"And that," said Saint slowly, "is your answer, son."

VI

LUCK found her father at home asleep, but her news was of such importance that she awoke him. He snarled an answer to her call before he realized who had called him.

"I've got a new teacher," she announced, when she had recovered from the effects of his snarling answer.

"Teacher, eh? Who?"

"The old man, with the white beard—Le Saint."

"Le—" Sleed sat up on the bed and stared at her.

Luck nodded. "Le Saint. He looks like one of the old men in the Bible. He is going to teach me, if you will let him."

Sleed stared down at the floor, with unseeing eyes, while Luck's words seemed to run in a meaningless jumble through his mind.

"We need a preacher here," said Luck softly, "and he is very good and kind. Will you let him teach me, Daddy?"

Sleed roused from his stupor and got heavily to his feet.

"Don't you feel good?" asked Luck. "Your face is so white and your eyes——"

"No, I'm all right!" grunted Sleed thickly. "I—I lost a lot of sleep, and this blasted heat—" He wiped his brow with the sleeve of his shirt.

"Are we going to live here always?" asked Luck.

"Always?" Sleed tried to smile. "Always is a long time, Luck."

Sleed picked up his hat and started for the door, but Luck took him by the arm.

"You did not say about my teacher."

Sleed did not look at her as he said, "When is he goin' to start teachin', Luck?"

"Tomorrow," eagerly.

"Oh, tomorrow. I reckon that'll be all right—tomorrow."

Sleed went out of the door and Luck watched him go down the rocky trail to the street, but he did not turn and wave at her as he usually did.

Suddenly he stopped, turned and came slowly back up the trail to the doorway.

"Luck, I wish you'd stay off the street tonight," he said.

"Why?" she asked. It was the first time he had ever requested her to keep away from the street.

"I'm afraid yuh might get hurt. There's a bunch comin' up from Cactus City tonight, and they might get rough. I can't afford to have anything happen to my Luck."

"They all know me," said Luck quickly. "Nothing will harm me."

Sleed shook his head.

"I—I dunno about that, Luck. If trouble started, nobody knows where bullets will hit."

Luck brushed the hair away from her eyes and glanced down toward the quiet street.

"Everybody says that you own Calico, Dad. If you do, why don't you stop the trouble? Does there have to be somebody killed every day? Isn't there some way to stop men from fighting and killing each other?"

Silver Sleed shook his head.

"No, I don't reckon there is, not now. Maybe some day the wolf blood will thin out, I dunno."

And without gaining Luck's promise to keep off the street that night, Sleed turned and went back down the trail. Luck watched him disappear and turned to see Mica Cates coming down past the house, on his way from the Ruby Hill trail.

He took off his hat and mopped his brow.

"Howdy, Miss Luck. Hot, ain't it? I been circ'latin' around quite a bit. Wes Marks jist run into a two-inch vein of durned-near pure silver. Could almost mint dollars out of the raw stuff. Two miners from the Nola had a devil of a fight and one's got a busted head.

"Didja notice how many buzzards has been floatin' around t'day? Been a whole flock of 'em circlin' Calico fer two hours. That old white-bearded hombre was settin' on a rock fer a long time, like he was thinkin' a heap, and then I seen him oilin' his six-gun. Mebbe he's a preacher; I dunno."

Mica Cates stopped for breath and glanced up at the sky, where a flock of buzzards circled slowly, and without visible effort. Cates lowered his eyes and glanced at Luck.

"'S hard to fool a buzzard," he said, and went on down the trail. He had fulfilled his duty and added a prophecy to boot.

Luck's eyes followed the buzzards for a while, as they circled slowly on an even plane, as though suspended by invisible wires, and went back into the house. There was something ominous in the atmosphere, and Luck had not given her word to keep off the street.

Loper had passed the word to Bill Fane and "Pecos" Mendez as to what Silver Sleed expected, and the three of them met in the Silver Bar saloon. Fane was a tall, cadaverous person, with a crooked mouth, which gave him a perpetual leer. Mendez was a half-breed, whose mentality was hardly up to par, but whose pistol ability and cold-blooded nerve were seldom equaled.

"We tak' care of de yong man, eh?" queried Mendez, his voice like the purring of a cat. "Dat be easy, eh, Beel?"

Fane nodded absently.

"No killin' is easy," objected Loper. "This young man packs a gun like he knowed how to use it, and he's got a face that backs up the looks of his gun. You two better figure that this ain't goin't' be no picnic."

"What does Sleed want 'em killed fer?" asked Fane.

"'Cause he don't 'low nobody to cut in on his gamblin' in Calico," replied Loper.

"He ain't never told 'em they can't run a game here, has he?"

"That's none of your business—nor mine," said Loper. "Silver Sleed pays yuh, don't he?"

"Yeah," admitted Fane slowly, "he pays. But I'm gittin' tired of bein' hired to shoot folks. I ain't no danged milk eater, Loper, but I believe in lettin' a man have a even break."

"You better not let Sleed hear yuh talk thataway," cautioned Loper. "He ain't got no use for that kind of arguments."

Fane grinned crookedly and put his hand on Loper's arm.

"Loper, who are we to let Silver Sleed hire us to do his dirty work? Why are we afraid of him? What did he ever do to make us afraid of him? Either one of us could bump him off with a gun. Are we afraid of his damn money?

"I got to lookin' him over today and wonderin' why we're afraid to speak out loud about him. You tell me not to let him hear me talk thataway. Why should I be any more afraid to let him hear it than you and Mendez?"

Loper drew away from Fane, but the question had found root in his brain.

"Money," said Mendez, "Just money. I jus' so good as Sleed, but Sleed has de money. Man got to live."

"I reckon that's it," nodded Loper. "I never thought much about it before, Bill. I reckon any of us could more than hold his own against Sleed in a gun-fight, but he's got the money. Anyway, I told him we'd take care of this for him."

The three of them strolled to the doorway. Far out on the desert was a strip of gold, marking the last of the sunset, but Calico was already hazy with the evening light. The Saint and Duke Steele came out of the Alley and into the street, walking slowly toward the Silver Bar saloon.

"Them is the ones," grunted Loper. "I dunno what Sleed wants done in case they don't open that game."

"He's doin' this 'cause he wants to stop 'em from gamblin', ain't he?" queried Fane. Loper nodded.

Mica Cates came thumping down the street and up to the saloon door, where he turned and looked up at the sky. He shaded his eyes for a moment and turned to the three men.

"Did yuh notice how the buzzards been hangin' around here all day?"

"What's that got to do with us?" grunted Loper.

"I dunno," admitted Cates. "I never said who it concerned. They've circled Calico all day, and sometimes they come down awful low, with their wattled heads turnin' from side to side—kinda lookin'." Cates shook his head and started into the saloon, but stopped and glanced at the sky again.

"'S hard to fool a buzzard, y'betcha."

"Croakin' old pup," growled Loper, and the three of them went back into the saloon.

The Saint secured his little table again and set it up in the street. Several dogs went out and investigated, and started a fight, as though there was a serious difference of opinion over the reasons for a table in the street.

Duke Steele watched the Saint with misgivings. He was sure that Silver Sleed would object strenuously to such a proceeding, but the Saint gave no heed to his warnings. For the last hour the Saint had seemed another person; entirely different from the philosophical old man. His mop of white hair seemed to lift aggressively, and the hawk-like nose seemed more like an eagle's beak.

He had put his extra cartridges in his pocket and shoved his six-shooter inside the waistband of his pants, where he could get it without reaching under his coat. Duke had noted these preparations silently, but had looked to his own gun and ammunition. He was willing to follow the Saint's lead and he wanted to be prepared for anything.

Duke went into the saloon and sat down at a poker table, where Sleed was dealing a game of stud. Sleed studied Duke from under the brim of his hat, as he slid a stack of chips across the table to him.

"The limit?" queried Duke.

"The sky," replied Sleed.

The Saint had split his winnings with Duke, and now Duke shoved the rest of the bills over to Sleed, taking chips in exchange. It was a small betting game, and the pots were uninteresting. Sleed covered a yawn with his hand, and Duke nodded, as though at a spoken word.

Duke smiled grimly as Sleed dealt the first card to each man. He shoved in part of a stack of chips, and Sleed covered the bet, wondering why Duke made such a bet on a hole-card. The two miners passed, leaving Sleed and Duke to fight it out. Duke drew a king and Sleed a jack.

"King-high bets," intoned Sleed.

Duke shoved in all of his chips. Sleed glanced sharply at him, but covered the bet, and dealt the rest of the hand. The result showed a pair of kings for Duke and a pair of jacks for Sleed.

The next deal doubled Duke's money again, and he bet half of it on his hole-card. Again he won. Sleed shifted nervously in his chair, while miners crowded in around to watch the play. Sleed knew that there was no chance for a crooked play, and he trusted to luck to win.

Pot after pot went to Duke Steele, doubling his money on each hand, until the onlookers gasped at the wonderful run of luck. Duke was plunging; betting a fortune on his first card. And Sleed's prestige in the town demanded that he follow suit, although it broke him.

Sleed called for another rack of chips, new cards, whiskey, praying that something would happen to break the devilish luck of this hard-eyed gambler.

Another deal, and Duke bet two thousand dollars on his first card. Sleed glanced at the bet and doubled the size of it.

"Feel it comin' on?" queried Duke. It was the first word Duke had spoken since he had inquired about the limit.

Sleed's eyes narrowed at the question, but he did not reply. Duke shoved in the extra two thousand, and with it went every chip in front of him. Stacks of blue and red, at five and ten dollars for each chip—a king's ransom. Sleed licked his lips and studied the pot.

"Your luck or mine," said Duke softly. "You're rich, Sleed, but are yuh game? It's a man-sized pot."

From out on the street came the voice of the Saint:

"It can't be beat, folks. The more you lay down, the less you pick up. The hand is quicker than the eye, and this game was designed to prove it to you. Don't bet, unless you want to lose."

Duke watched Sleed closely, as he stared down at the pot.

"It's luck that wins, Sleed; and you're losin' your luck."

"What do you mean?" snapped Sleed, sitting up straight in his chair. "What do you mean?"

"She's leavin' you, Sleed. You know it, too. Shove in your money and prove it with the cards. It's luck now. I'll show you my card."

Duke flipped his hole-card, disclosing a deuce of hearts.

"The little thin card, Sleed. Your card must be as good as mine; but my luck—my medicine—is stronger than yours. Your luck has left you."

"Like hell it has!" croaked Sleed, and turned his card, the ace of spades, face up on the table. Nervously he shoved in chips, calling for another rack to match Duke's bet.

"Deal 'em face-up," said Duke softly. "Give the crowd a little entertainment, Sleed."

"Another empty shell," came the Saint's voice. "This is not a luck game, folks; it is a cinch for the dealer."

Sleed's hand shook as he started to deal. Duke got an ace, while Sleed's card showed the five of hearts. Slowly the next two fell to the table; a five of clubs to Duke and the deuce of diamonds to Sleed.

"Ace, five, deuce," said Duke softly. "Luck is laughing at you, Sleed."

Sleed tossed the next two, and the crowd gasped. Each man drew a king.

"Matched cards," said Duke, laughing softly. "One more card, Sleed, one more. This one proves that luck has left you."

Slowly Sleed moved the top card and tossed it across at Duke. It was the deuce of clubs, making a pair of deuces for Duke Steele. An ace, king, or a five would win for Sleed.

"Friend, you are out of luck." The Saint's voice seemed to be directed at Silver Sleed. "I told you that this game cannot be beat, but you——"

Sleed spun his card in the air and it fell face-up on the pile of chips.

The trey of spades!

Staring down at the card, Sleed half-slumped forward in his chair, as he tried to estimate his loss. It was more money than he dared estimate. He looked up at Duke, who was rolling a cigarette.

"Count the chips, Sleed," said Duke, "and give me your I. O. U. for it. I'll take your count."

Duke got to his feet and brushed the crumbs of tobacco off the folds of his shirt, while Sleed stared up at him. His I. O. U.! Sleed's eyes shifted and he saw Loper looking at him inquiringly. Swiftly Sleed counted the chips, stacking them in rows across the table.

"Forty-six thousand dollars," he said hoarsely.

"Write it out," said Duke indifferently.

Sleed got to his feet and walked to the bar, where he secured writing material. Laboriously he wrote out the I. O. U. and scrawled his signature at the bottom. Without looking at it, Duke pocketed it and went out of the door.

Loper and Fane had moved in close to the bar, and as Duke went out of the door, Sleed nodded to Loper and indicated for him to go ahead. Men were talking softly about the big game, the size of Sleed's loss, the cold nerve of this stranger. A rumble of it came to Sleed's ears and he grinned behind his beard. He was sure that he would never have to pay that I. O. U.

Voices came from the street arguing, laughing, quarreling. Sleed had turned away, as though to go toward the back of the room, but he swung around and walked to the door, drawn irresistibly by the drama he knew was about to be played.

VII

THE Saint was standing at his little table, in the center of a crowd, advising them not to play his game; taking their money, when they insisted. Duke Steele had elbowed his way to a point just beyond the Saint, and was watching the crowd.

Loper shoved men aside and stepped in front of the table, looking curiously down at the two shells. Duke had seen Sleed signal Loper in the saloon, and he knew that Loper was the one who had killed Ace Ault. Loper was Sleed's man, and this was their first move against the Saint.

"Don't waste your money, friend," warned the Saint, as Loper took out some gold. "You can't win."

"Can, if I pick the right shell, can't I?"

"That's the trick, friend, but it can't be done."

The Saint rolled the little black pea on the table, covered it with a shell and shuffled the shells slowly.

"Fifty dollars," declared Loper.

"Pick your shell," said the Saint. "Fifty is a lot of money to give away."

Loper studied the shells for a moment and made his choice. The pea was not there. With a swift movement of his hand he upset the other shell and found it empty.

He stepped back angrily.

"That's a crooked game!" he roared. "You just stole my money——"

Loper drew his gun as he rasped out his accusation, which was never finished. The Saint's hand flashed to his waist; a downward and upward movement, so fast that it seemed to be one short snap, and his pistol spouted fire a second before Loper shot.

Loper jerked back as though struck by a mighty blow and his bullet sped harmlessly over the Saint's head. For an instant the crowd was silent. Loper had half caught his balance, but it was only an instant before he fell forward on his face.

Into the startled crowd came Luck, running swiftly to the Saint.

"Look out, Saint!" yelled Duke. "It's a trick to kill you."

Another pistol thudded from nearer the saloon, and the Saint staggered sideways from the shock of the bullet. It was Mendez shooting from the sidewalk. Duke sprang into a cleared spot and fired twice at Mendez, who tried to run, but seemed to collapse half-way in the saloon door, at the feet of Silver Sleed.

The street cleared as though by magic, and Duke could see the Saint on his hands and knees beside his little table, trying to pull himself up. A woman screamed and a man cursed wonderingly in a high-pitched voice.

As Duke started for the Saint, he felt a bullet yank at his shoulder, and the crash of a gun came from behind him. He turned quickly to see Bill Fane coming toward him. Fane shot again before Duke realized that here was another opponent, and the bullet seared a furrow across his cheek.

Duke's hand swung up and he fired quickly. Fane stumbled, but came on, trying to lift his gun, which seemed too heavy. Again Duke fired—and again. Fane's gun fell to the ground. He seemed to be looking for it, searching carefully. His knees bent slowly and he sprawled in the street.

Duke turned around. The Saint had got to his feet and was holding to the table with both hands. Men were looking out of the saloon door, standing far back from the doorway, as though afraid to get closer to the street.

Loper was sprawled on his face just in front of the Saint, and had not moved. Duke went past him and took the Saint by the arm. His white hair and beard were covered with blood, and his eyes were closed tightly.

"Come on, Saint," said Duke. "Aw, this is a hell of a mess, ain't it? Are yuh hurt bad?"

The Saint mumbled something in his beard, but let Duke lead him off the street, between two of the buildings. Behind them came the sound of voices, as the people came back into the street. Duke led the Saint around the rear of the buildings, until he struck the trail into the Alley. His face was bleeding and a dull pain in his shoulder apprised him of the fact that the first bullet had torn through the flesh.

The Saint mumbled incoherent sentences, but led the way to their shack, where he sat down on a rock and held his head in his hands. Duke tried to examine the Saint's injuries, but the old man shoved him away, mumbling a curse.

Duke squinted closely at him. It was the first time he had ever heard the Saint curse.

"You sure got hit hard, pardner," observed Duke. "I don't reckon yuh never swore because yuh didn't know how."

From the street came the sound of voices, as though the crowd had separated and was searching; scattered voices yelling instructions, with one group closer than the rest. Duke reloaded his pistol and shook the Saint's shoulder.

"Get up, Saint! There's men comin', and we don't know whether they're friends or not."

But the Saint mumbled thickly and shook his head. Came a scraping noise at the doorway, and Duke lifted his head to see Luck leaning inside.

"Come out!" she panted excitedly. "They are coming to hang you both! Hurry!"

Duke yanked the Saint to his feet and shoved him out of the doorway. The silhouetted figures of men were coming over the rim of the Alley toward them.

"Follow me!" whispered Luck. "It's your only chance."

The Saint mumbled thickly and tried to protest, but Duke hustled him along in the heavy shadow of the rock ledges, while behind them came the clamor of voices, like a pack of hounds casting for a scent.

Luck led them angling up the side of the hill, over ledges where Duke had to fairly carry the Saint, until they came out over the rim. Below them shone the yellow lights of the street, which seemed to be deserted now. From down in Sunshine Alley came the faint voices of the searchers, calling to each other; voices that echoed strangely from that black cleft in the mountain.

Luck took them straight to her own home. The Saint sat down on the door-step and held his head in his hands, while he began his incoherent mumble again.

"Whose place is this?" asked Duke.

"Mine," panted Luck. "Bring him inside."

"Your home? Silver Sleed's place?"

"Yes. Don't you see it's the only place where they won't search?"

"But suppose they do," argued Duke. "What will they think of you, Miss Luck?"

"They won't come here. Help him inside, please. They will think you hid in the rocks tonight. I know a trail that leads around Ruby Hill and you can go out that way into the desert. Nobody will ever think of watching that trail.

"I'll get your burro and the stuff from your shack. Bring him in before some of them pass here. They may search the hill tonight."

Duke helped the Saint to his feet and shoved him into the doorway. Luck dropped the heavy blanket curtain over the front window and lit some candles, while Duke guided the Saint to a chair.

The old man's hair and beard were a clotted mass of red and white now, and his eyes blinked painfully in the candle-light. He tried to get to his feet, but Duke put a hand on his shoulder.

"The traps," mumbled the Saint, "I'm going to take up the traps, Jim."

"What does he mean?" whispered Luck.

"Out of his head," said Duke. "That bullet must have cracked his skull."

The Saint looked curiously at Duke.

"Are you from St. Pierre?" he asked.

"He don't know you," whispered Luck.

The Saint bowed his head for a moment and then looked back at Duke.

"Did they find her?" he whispered hoarsely. "Did they?"

"Take it easy, pardner," soothed Duke.

"I'll have to get yuh out of here ahead of a rope. They ain't lookin' for her; they're lookin' for us."

"My father sent me home," explained Luck. "I ran out of the street when the shooting began and he grabbed me. He was very angry and made me come home. The—the men who got shot were friends of my father.

"But I didn't come home—then," she continued, after a moment's pause. "I heard them say they were going to hang you both."

"We're sure obliged to yuh, Miss Luck," said Duke slowly. "We'll get out of here before they find yuh out."

Came a dull knock on the heavy door. Duke drew his gun and stepped in closer to the wall, snuffing out one of the candles.

"I'll open it," he whispered, but Luck motioned him to stop.

"Who is it?" she called.

"Me—Mica Cates," answered a muffled voice. "You paw asked me to find out if yuh was home."

"I'm all right," said Luck.

"I'll tell him. They ain't found them fellers yet, Luck; but they're still huntin'. Your dad is willin' to pay big for the man what gets 'em. Loper's dead. Mendez and Fane are kinda bad, but mebbe they'll live."

For a moment there was silence, and then Cates said, "'Member what I said about them buzzards? It sure is hard to fool a buzzard. G'd-night."

Luck turned to Duke, her face white in the flickering light of the one candle.

"My dad," she said slowly, "is offering money for your lives."

Duke thought of the I. O. U. in his pocket. Forty-six thousand dollars. No wonder Silver Sleed was willing to pay well to stop collection on that piece of paper. It would break Sleed to pay that bet; strip him of his unearned wealth.

"I reckon your dad's got the wrong idea of us," said Duke slowly. He did not want her to know why Silver Sleed wanted to kill him.

"I'll get your burro and things," she said, and slipped out through the back entrance before he could stop her. The Saint lifted his gory head and stared at her as she went past him. He started to get up, but sank back in his chair, muttering softly, wonderingly.

He looked at Duke closely, without a sign of recognition in his eyes.

"How do yuh feel, Saint?" asked Duke.

"How do I feel?" parroted the Saint. "Why do you ask me that? Where am I?"

"Don't yuh remember, Saint? You're in Silver Sleed's home right now."

"Sleed's home?" The Saint got slowly out of his chair and looked around, as though an inspection of the four walls would corroborate his statement.

"Sleed's home?" he repeated, as though to himself and then to Duke. "I don't understand—I—can't."

"Don't yuh remember the shootin' in the street? One of Sleed's men shot yuh, Saint; but he paid damn well for it."

"One of Sleed's men? What men do you mean?"

It was not the voice of the old Saint. Gone was the deep, organ-like tone, and in its place was a harsh, rasping enunciation, toneless, colorless.

"You take it easy, old timer," advised Duke. "We'll get out of here first and talk afterwards."

The Saint heard this indifferently, as his hand ran slowly through his great white beard, now streaked and clotted with blood. Across the room was a mirror in a rough frame, and his eyes traveled to this. He staggered over to it and peered at himself for several long moments.

He turned away and staggered against the wall, where he stared at Duke, wide-eyed.

"Who am I?" he breathed. "My God, who am I?"

His voice was almost a scream, and his hands clutched against the rough wall. There was no doubt in Duke's mind but that the Saint had gone insane from his wound.

"Easy, pardner," soothed Duke. "You'll remember who yuh are. Set down and take it easy."

"Who am I?" whined the Saint, paying no heed to Duke's advice. "Don't you know whom I am?"

"Le Saint," answered Duke.

"Yes, that's my name—Le Saint."

He stared at Duke for several moments, shaking his head as though in pain or perplexity. Then he said, "I don't know you, but your face is familiar. Who are you?"

"Duke Steele."

"Yes," nodded the Saint, "that is the name, but I don't remember you very well. You heard what happened to me, didn't you?" The question was child-like in its simplicity, and the Saint smiled wistfully as he spoke.

"What happened to you?" queried Duke.

"I thought everyone knew. The factor at Norway Lake told everyone—I—thought."

"Where's Norway Lake?"

The Saint smiled and shook his head.

"I forgot that you were a stranger. It is north of here. I am a trapper; a free trader, they call me. There were three of us on Moose River—no, four. But there were only three of us went in there. The baby was born that winter.

"The fur was plentiful and our catch was large. My wife—" The Saint stopped and stared at the floor, as though unable to continue.

"It was a hard life for a woman, away from her own kind. I trusted my partner." The Saint's manner seemed to change, and he cursed witheringly in a mixture of English, French and another language, which Duke had never heard. It seemed to relieve him, for he continued:

"The fur was ready to take out in the spring, and my partner was to make the voyage alone. On the day he left, I was going to take up a few traps which had not been lifted. Somehow, my wife seemed nervous, and I questioned her. She confessed that she was afraid of my partner.

"I laughed. My friend, it seemed a huge joke. The load of furs was launched and my partner waved adieu. I watched him pole away and went to my wife, laughing at her grave expression.

"'He is gone,' I said, 'and anyway it is foolish of you to feel as you do about him. Has he ever been anything except a good friend to us?'

"'I do not know,' she replied, as she hugged the baby and went into the cabin. I laughed and went on the trail. But a man's mind is the devil's garden, where seeds of suspicion take root easily, and I grew uneasy. I would go back to the little cabin and stay with my wife until she was no longer afraid.

"I reached the cabin just in time to see my partner, who had returned, forcing my wife into the canoe. He had come back, evidently with the intention of stealing my wife along with the furs.

"I shouted at him as I ran down the shore, and I saw him throw my baby bodily into the canoe with my wife, who had fainted from her struggle. And then he shoved off from the shore, just as I reached there, but not soon enough to escape."

The Saint drew his hand across his eyes, as though striving to shut out that sight.

"We fought," he continued slowly, "fought like beasts, and I whipped him, but just before he went down under a powerful blow he managed to fall against the canoe and shove it into the current, where the water gains speed for the white rapids below."

The Saint shook his head slowly.

"I never found them—never. I forgot the man who was responsible for my loss, and he escaped. I have sworn to kill him, my friend. The Indians found the overturned canoe—empty."

"For God's sake!" breathed Duke, as the Saint bowed his head over a loss sustained twenty years before. It seemed utterly impossible—yet true.

"What was your partner's name?" asked Duke.

"Martin," replied the Saint evenly, through clenched teeth.

Duke shook his head. He knew no one by the name. He knew little about the loss of memory, but felt sure that the bullet, which had scored the Saint's head, had shocked him back twenty years, and he shuddered as he wondered what must be the Saint's feeling when he realized that he had lost twenty years of his life.

From below the cabin came the hoarse yelling of a man, like the leader of a wolf-pack sounding a view hello to his comrades when he scents the trail anew. Shouts answered him.

Suddenly the back door crashed open and Luck half-fell inside, panting painfully.

"They know where you are!" she panted. "I got your burro and blankets, but they found me and took them away. Someone made a guess that you were at my house, and my father struck him down for the suggestion, but they are coming to find out."

"I reckon we'll meet 'em here," said Duke slowly, and nodded toward the Saint.

"He's gone crazy, Luck."

As Luck looked toward the Saint he raised his head and looked straight at Duke, as he said, "Who has gone crazy, Duke?"

It was the booming voice of the old Saint again. He got to his feet and shook his head, as though to clear his befogged memory.

"They're cornerin' us, Saint," said Duke, "and it kinda looks like the end of the trail."

"Come out this way—quick!" urged Luck, starting for the rear door, which opened on to a rocky slope, leading on a steep grade up the side of Ruby Hill. The Saint stumbled out of the door, with Duke close behind him, and they went up the hill, winding their way around the tall spires, dodging from shadow to shadow to escape the moonlight, which lighted the world like a mighty blue-tinted, incandescent lamp.

Behind them came the voices of the mob, the crashing of the front door of the cabin, hollow, muffled voices, as those inside shouted the information that their quarry had escaped from the rear.

"The tunnels!" panted Luck. "The hill is full of them."

They stopped for a breathing spell and watched the crowd below them climbing the hill, their voices plainly audible in the thin atmosphere.

"They're headin' for the tunnels!" shouted Silver Sleed's voice. "We'll get 'em now!"

Duke turned and followed Luck, climbing higher and higher over the barren rocks, while below them came the redoubled shouts of the crowd, as they saw the flitting figures far up on the cliffs.

"The Saint!" exclaimed Duke suddenly. "Where is he?"

Luck, panting against a rock, looked back. She and Duke were alone. Breathlessly they scanned the world below them, and watched the crowd coming; black figures in that ghostly light.

All danger to themselves was forgotten. What had become of the Saint?

"He's crazy," muttered Duke. "That bullet knocked him crazy, but he's my pardner and I'm going back, Luck."

"They kill you!" panted Luck. "My father——"

But Duke Steele was going back down the hill, calling softly the Saint's name and Luck followed him. There was no sign of him in the path of the coming crowd, so Duke and Luck swung wide, peering into the shadows, until they were almost past the mob, which had not seen them return.

"Gawd!" muttered Duke. "If we could find him now we could double back on them."

Suddenly the clamoring crowd went silent. It was uncanny. Duke led the way swiftly around the base of a broken ledge and they found themselves just at the rear of the halted mob, a mob as silent as the dead.

Just beyond and above them stood the Saint, a huge figure, back-lighted in the moonlight until it seemed that a halo encircled his great, white head. Silently, like a prophet of old; he reared his huge bulk in their path, as though rebuking them for their evil actions.

Duke caught his breath. It was so unreal, weird.

"Kill him!" grunted Silver Sleed's voice, but the crowd did not move. It was as though the Saint held a strange power over them. Duke gripped his gun tightly and waited. There was nothing he could do to help the Saint now.

Then, slowly, the Saint began his descent toward the crowd, which parted to let him through. Miners, hardened gamblers, killers, the riff-raff of the new West, drew aside in wonderment or fear of this man.

Slowly he came among them, peering into their faces, as though seeking someone, while they silently stared at him.

"Blood!" muttered Mica Cates, who was near Duke and the girl. "Blood and buzzards."

Suddenly the Saint stopped. He was looking straight at Silver Sleed now, and Silver Sleed's right hand held a cocked pistol at his hip, tensed, ready to fire. Then the Saint spoke:

"The trail ends here, Sleed Martin. It has been full of shadows, and I have only a memory—just a memory. I want you, whom men call Silver Sleed. It may only be a nightmare, Martin, but it is real to me—now!"

As the Saint spoke he sprang, like a tiger. Silver Sleed fired, but his bullet smashed into the cliff behind the Saint, and before he could shoot again, the Saint was upon him.

Both of them were giant men, and they crashed together like two grizzlies, while the crowd backed away to give them room, knowing nothing of the reasons for the fight. Luck had started ahead, but Duke drew her back against the rock.

"My God, he's stronger than Sleed!" gasped a man. "Look at him, will yuh?"

The rest of the crowd watched silently the stranger battle. Silver Sleed was battling for his life while the old Saint, insane with the stored-up hate of years, and with the super-human strength of a madman, battered and crushed Silver Sleed without mercy.

The thudding of mighty blows, the crash of clinches, scraping of feet on the barren rock; but no sound from the mob. For all the movement about them, they might as well have been fighting alone on the mountain top.

Suddenly they drew apart, only to crash together again, but this time Silver Sleed went down, striking the back of his head against the rock. The Saint stood over him, hunched, with arms bent, like the wings of an eagle about to strike, then his arms swept down around Silver Sleed and swung up, with Sleed in his arms. With a mighty heave he swung the unconscious man across his shoulder, turned and lumbered away around the side of the cliffs.

"Stop him!" screamed a man.

"Stop him!" echoed the crowd, suddenly realizing that they had voices. After him they went, but the chase was slow. It was only a narrow trail, which broke off to the sharp cliffs below it. Beyond them went the Saint, with the sure-footedness of a mountain goat, traveling at a pace that none dared imitate.

Duke and Luck followed closely. Duke had forgotten that he was also being hunted by the crowd, and it is doubtful if any of the crowd knew or cared about him now.

"He's got to go into the Silver Shell tunnel!" yelled a man. "That's the end of the trail."

Beyond this tunnel was a wide crevice in the cliffs, which extended back into the mountain. It was impossible to go beyond the tunnel, either up or down. The Saint had trapped himself. Stumbling along this trail came the crowd, or as many as dared to trust this narrow pathway in the tricky moonlight until they reached the wide ledge which constituted the mouth of the Silver Shell.

"He's bottled up," cried a miner, "but it ain't goin' to help Sleed none!"

"There's a cross-cut tunnel into the Kalura," panted a newcomer. "He'll find that. Watch the mouth of the Kalura, I tell yuh!"

The crowd ran back along the trail, until they could look up and beyond the crevice, where the Kalura workings opened out onto a much higher ledge. From this spot it was five hundred feet straight down into Sunshine Alley.

A man cocked his rifle and leaned back against the rocky wall, but another jerked the gun away from him.

"You fool! Killin' the old man won't save Sleed, and you can't be sure in this light."

Suddenly two figures appeared on this ledge, silhouetted against the moon. Sleed had recovered from his injury and was fighting again. They clashed together, blending into one figure. Then the Saint picked Sleed up in his arms, balanced him for a second, and hurled him far out over the abyss.

The man with the rifle dropped it and flung his hands to his eyes, and a hoarse gasp went up from the crowd as Sleed's body faded out into the depths, falling like a plummet.

The Saint was standing near the edge of the rock, with his arms high above his head as he gazed into space. Then his laughter came down to them, the choking cackle of a maniac. It was the first time that Duke Steele had ever heard the Saint laugh aloud.

Luck was leaning back against the rock, her face as white as snow and with her eyes shut. For a moment Duke thought she had fainted, but her eyes opened and she stared back at the old Saint atop the ledge, still cackling in his glee.

As he lowered his arms and turned, as though to go back into the tunnel, he slipped, fell sidewise, clawing at the rock, which slid away with him. For a moment he seemed to hang, half-off the cliff, but the edge of the rock seemed to crumble away under his weight, and he shot sidewise into space to join Silver Sleed.

Duke had started forward, as though to try and help the Saint, and when he turned back, Luck was gone. Silently the crowd filed past him, wordless from the tragedy they had just seen, forgetting that he was one of the men they had been hunting.

Duke gazed for a long time into the silvered depths of the Alley. From far away came the eerie, wailing cry of a desert coyote. Duke shook his head. Perhaps it was better for the Saint. Memory had only half returned to him; the balancing point which might mean insanity. He had achieved his purpose after twenty years; twenty years of another personality, which urged him on to hunt down the man who had ruined his life. Suddenly Duke realized that Luck was the daughter of the Saint. She had been the lost baby. Sleed was Sleed Martin, the trapping partner of the Saint.

"Twenty years another person," muttered Duke. "My Gawd! No wonder he looked in that glass and asked me who he was!"

Duke turned and went slowly down the hill toward Sleed's cabin. A gray burro crossed into the moonlight; Duke's burro. It was half-packed and dragging a blanket. The pack-sacks were still intact, half-filled with food, and a small keg of water was tied between the saddle-posts. Luck had made good as far as she was able.

Duke caught the animal and led it down the hill behind him. He did not know where he was going now. Near the corner of Sleed's home he stopped. Someone was talking, and Duke recognized Mica Cates's voice. Duke edged in closer.

Luck was sitting on the rough steps, with her head buried in her hands, while Mica Cates and another man stood near her.

"It shore was hard luck," said Mica softly, "but I knowed somethin' was due to happen."

"But why?" sobbed Luck. "Why did that man do it?"

"Crazy," grunted Mica.

"He called him Martin. My daddy's name was Sleed."

"He wa'n't responsible, Luck," said the other man. "He was jist plumb crazy, thasall."

"Don't yuh worry," soothed Cates. "Calico'll take care of yuh. Why, yo're rich, Luck. Everythin' yore dad had belongs to you. You can git eddicated and have silk dresses, and—" Mica Cates seemed to expand—"and you won't have t' live in Calico."

"What become of that other feller?" queried the other man. "I reckon we plum forgot him. Sleed wanted him especially. I wonder if he wasn't crazy, too?"

Luck looked up quickly.

"Don't say that. He—he wasn't crazy."

Duke turned away and picked up the lead-rope of his burro, and went softly around the house and down past the lighted town, which was strangely silent for Calico.

A few miles out on the desert he stopped and looked back at the lights of Calico, which were now only a tiny flicker against the dead black of the hills. Slowly he drew out a folded paper from his pocket and looked at the scrawl thereon:

I owe you forty-six thousand dollars.
$46,000.00
Silver Sleed.

Duke glanced back at Calico as he slowly tore the paper into bits and scattered them to the wind. He picked up the lead-rope and spoke softly to the burro.

"One man wondered if I was crazy, and she denied it. Forty-six thousand dollars. I wonder which was right?"

And he turned and went into the misty spaces of the desert—alone.

Milton Keynes UK
Ingram Content Group UK Ltd.
UKHW012315040624
443649UK00007B/651